The No Nonsense

Woman's Guide To

Setting Up A

Business

by

Bernadette Jones

First Published 2013 by HLS Publishing Solutions

ISBN: 1490310371

Copyright © 2012 by Bernadette Jones

Who is Bernadette Jones?

Bernadette started her own business in 2008, after having worked as a PA/Secretary for over thirty years. Alongside her on site secretarial and virtual administration support framework, Bernadette also provides business mentoring to women new to business, based purely on her own personal experiences:-

"I was truly inspired by Berni after our first meeting. She had built her own successful business as a virtual assistant and not only was her business thriving but she had so many ideas on where to take her business next. She had real passion. This initial meeting planted the seed in my mind that I could become a virtual assistant too. I have now started my own business and asked Berni if she would be my mentor. Berni has been with me through my ups and downs and she has been so helpful and supportive. She is very approachable and friendly and not too far away when you need her. If you are thinking about a mentoring service, I would recommend Berni without hesitation. You will not be disappointed."

Madeleine Price – Home PA Services,

www.homepaservices.co.uk

"I met Berni through a mutual networking contact. Having worked in the admin field for over 25 years I needed help to understand the context and capabilities of social media to promote my new business. In our session Berni broke down the barriers of fear and uncertainty and stripped away the technical jargon. The session left me with a complete and concise framework which I am now able to use confidently to build my social media profiles. I would have no hesitation in recommending Berni as a Mentor for business start up's."

San Stockhall – Fox Executive,

www.foxexecutive.co.uk

Contents

Introduction

Well done on taking the first steps towards setting up your own business. I am here to guide you through the entire process from initial idea to a real-life working business run by you.

I know how scary and exciting this step can be. I've done it myself. I left the rat-race, the corporate world and set up my own business as a virtual assistant. I'm now my own boss, choosing my own hours, choosing my own clients and making my own profits. It wasn't easy, but with help and support I did it and I want you to do it too. Whether you want to be a virtual assistant, set up your own online or offline business, or become a freelancer in whatever field you choose, this guide is for you.

Why Write a Guide Just for Women?

When I started out in business, I found that most of the advice out there was aimed at men; there was very little aimed at women. Yet all over the world women are starting more and more businesses.

In the UK alone 12% more women started up their own businesses in 2011 than in 2010. Women are now responsible for 37% of all UK start-ups. In the United States, the Women's Business Momentum Centre reports that the largest group of business start-ups are women.

Despite this, most of the advice you see is aimed at men. Yet women in business do have different needs, different problems to solve and need a different way of doing business. This guide will help you with those differences and help to set you on your way to running your own business.

In this guide we will look at:

- Coming up with a business idea.

- Finding a name for your business.

- Creating the correct work-life balance.

- Arranging funding for your business.

- Sorting out a place to work.

- Dealing with the tax man.

- Networking for women in business and much, much more.

Ready? Let's get started.

Why Start Up Your Own Business?

Whilst not many people would dare ask a man that question, you will find you are asked it a LOT as a woman.

There are lots of reasons why you might decide to start up your own business. Here are just a few of them:

- You are in control of your working hours - ideal for the working mum or carer.

- You are in control of your job - you won't have someone else dumping their work on you.

- You get to do what you want to do - most of the time anyway - you do still have to do some boring things, but more on that later.

- It is challenging and exciting - and sometimes we all need some of that!

- It can be very profitable - you set your rates, you determine your hours, you decide what you earn!

- It is varied - No two days will ever be the same!

- You'll learn new skills and meet lots of new people.

- No more commuting!

- You are your boss!

There are lots of positives to starting your own business. I know the women I've spoken to would never go back to working for someone else. However, they and I also know that, just like romance, it's not all roses and champagne when setting up in business.

There are some downsides too, the most common ones being:

- Time to set up a new business.

- Costs of setting up a new business.

- Loneliness of the Self-Employed Woman.

This guide will show you how to deal with the downsides and make the most of the positives of starting your own business.

Can You Afford to Start Up Your Own Business?

I don't mean to be crass, but can you afford not to? Working for yourself gives you so much more freedom and a sense of satisfaction you will never get working for someone else. However, starting up a business does cost money, how much and how to fund it depends upon the business you wish to set-up and your current situation.

For example, as a virtual assistant my initial costs were quite low. I needed a decent computer, internet connection and a website. A freelance writer I know started with just a laptop and an internet connection. She got her website hosted for free by doing some copywriting work for a hosting company. She wasn't a writer before she started her own business; she used to work in a primary school before she had her children and needed a job she could fit in around them.

A nail technician I know had most of her equipment from when she trained at college, her start up costs were some more polish and equipment, leaflets and advertising.

The thing is, it doesn't cost as much to start-up your business as you might be led to believe. Some sites talk about legal fees, website fees, printing fees, equipment and stationery and can scare you with 'facts' like setting up your business will run into thousands of pounds.

Fact: If you're starting up as a sole-trader in the UK (See The Right Structure) it costs NOTHING to set up in business - there are no legal fees. Websites can be hosted for next to nothing and easily designed yourself using a free template. You don't need printed stationery to set up in business - you can use word processing software to make your own. And you can, if you need to, work from your kitchen table or from the back of your car. You don't need offices or office furniture.

You can, generally, in most business areas get started for a few hundred pounds. We will look at ways to raise funding in: Business Plans and Getting Funding.

You don't even need to start out full-time. Many successful start-ups begin as part-time businesses whilst the owner makes contacts, gets sales and gets more finance in place before she takes the leap to full-time self-employment.

The thing that some guides won't tell you; it's actually much easier and much more affordable to start up in business than you have been led to believe.

This is something that women all over the world are starting to wake up to, which is why more businesses are being started by women every year. Working for yourself is the perfect working solution for most women.

You owe it to yourself to see if it is the perfect solution for you too.

What do you have to lose?

Choosing a Business

This is something that only you can do, I'm afraid. If you want to start up your own business but have no idea what you'd like to do, you might benefit from attending one of my workshops where I can talk to you personally and advise you on suitable options.

Generally, I advise people to choose something they either:

- Know and understand

- Want to do passionately

And that there is a market for! You are in this for money as well as love!

Here are just a few of the many start-up businesses women have begun in the past twelve months:

Virtual Assistant	Personal Trainer
Freelance Writer	Chef
Freelance Proof-reader	Set up a local business magazine
Freelance Photographer	Set up a PR agency
E-bay Business	Set up a cake making service
Selling books on Amazon/EBay	Will-writing service
Mobile Hairdresser	Accountant
Mobile Nail Technician	Book-keeper
Mobile Beauty Therapist	Nutritionist
Cleaning service	IT support
Ironing service	Set up an organic herb company
Concierge Service	Web-design business
Dog-Walking Service	Web-based business
Child-minding	Translation service
Events Planner	Sandwich delivery service

When it comes to choosing your business, you must do what you want to do!

What's In a Name?

Everything! You need a business name that is professional but unique to you. You also need one that cannot easily be confused with another better known brand or company.

Your name might well be Wendy Hazel Smith, but you cannot set up in business as W.H. Smith! Bernadette and Quinzel cannot trade as B&Q!

This is known as 'passing-off' and will not be viewed as amusing by the large companies, or their lawyers, or by you when your business is closed and you have to change your name and pay damages!

So choose wisely.

You can brainstorm with friends and family or just write names onto slips of paper and pull them out.

Do whatever works for you. You might want to run the potential name for your business past your family and friends for their opinion - but that is not compulsory - remember this is YOUR business - your baby - you get to choose it all!

If you are having difficulty in choosing a name, I offer help and tips in my workshop for women starting up in business.

When you are choosing the name for your business it is a good idea, in fact some would say it is essential, to check for websites already using your intended name before you decide upon a name for your business.

You don't want to choose a name, set everything up and then discover that the website for your chosen company name already exists and sells something completely inappropriate or is in direct competition with you!

So, before you go too far along the name game, you need to also think about your website.

Websites - Not a Luxury but a Necessity

To do business in the 21st Century, no matter what your business is, you will need a website. If you're a dog walker, a personal trainer, make wedding cakes, plan weddings or write wills - you need a website to advertise your services to potential clients.

Think about it! You use the web all the time to look for things - so do your potential clients.

So if you are going to succeed, you will need a web presence, a basic web site at least.

The first thing you need to do is to find a suitable domain name for your business.

This is where the name of your business and your website has to be chosen together.

Go to a domain name service such as:

http://www.lcn.com/ or

http://www.godaddy.com/ or

http://order.1and1.co.uk/

And type in your preferred business name or web name into the search button.

See if the names you want are still available.

If not, think again and then search your new business name.

When you find a name you like, that your friends and family think is good (optional) and that you can buy the domain name for (not-optional) then you need to buy that domain name.

WARNING! Check the prices of the domains at each of the domain name sites as these can vary considerably. It is often much cheaper to buy two years' domain name ownership than one.

You are advised to purchase not just the .co.uk domain, but also the .com and .net or .biz as a minimum. This is to prevent people buying up similar domain names to yours and then setting up a porn site which they will only take down if you 'buy' the site from them. This happens!

Website Hosting

You can either buy hosting from the domain name company (which is the easiest option) or you can look for hosting from other providers. This depends upon how IT literate you are.

One advantage for the not so IT literate of using the hosting from the domain companies is that they also often come with easy to use WYSIWYG (What You See is What You Get) web editors, which make it easy to get your website up and running.

No-cost Website Hosting

If you are offering a freelance service of interest to business, such as web design, graphic designer, writer, virtual assistant, data entry, translation etc. you can have a free 'mini' site hosted by many of the online job bidding sites such as http://www.elance.com and http://www.vworker.com. These mini-sites are not ideal, but are a good, no-cost alternative for those working in relevant freelance industries.

Website Content

What should I put on my website?

As a basic minimum you need to show clients:

- what you do

- who you are

- where you are based

- how they can contact you.

As your business develops and grows you might want to put in client testimonials and samples of your work (photos of cakes you've made, nail designs, articles, web pages etc.)

Do not rush your website content.

This is your salesman, 24 hours a day, 7 days a week, 365 days a year. It needs to be perfect!

- Do not make it too cluttered.

- Don't go for too many colours or fonts.

- Do add appropriate images (you can get hold of royalty free photos for websites and stationery at Stock Xching (http://www.sxc.hu/signup)

- Do double and triple check it for spelling and grammatical errors.

- Do check it is easy and clear to read.

- Do ensure it is professional.

- If in any doubt, hire a copywriter to either check your site for you or to write the content for your site.

- Do check it works in all browsers! (This sounds very techy but it is easy to do.

Simply go to http://browsershots.org/ type in your URL (your web address) and it will show you how it looks in all browsers.

Take a look at other websites of small businesses in the same industry area as you to get an idea of what to do and more importantly what not to do and then design your own website.

Do not, however, copy any text directly from a competitor's website. This is not only extremely unprofessional, it is theft. In the internet it is known as plagiarism and the penalty for plagiarism can be to have your site shut down!

Get Connected

Once your website is up and running, you need to let people know about it. Mention it on your Facebook page, your Twitter account and email your friends and family. Get your website name printed onto business cards, leaflets etc.

But, also, get your site listed on Google Bing and the other search engines.

Google:

http://www.google.co.uk/submit_content.html

Bing:

https://ssl.bing.com/webmaster/SubmitSitePage.aspx

Yahoo!

http://help.yahoo.com/l/us/yahoo/directory/suggest/

You can also use site submitting services if you wish.

I take a closer look at websites, web promotion, web marketing and web content in my workshop for women starting up in business.

Search Engine Optimisation (SEO)

You can pay SEO experts to help get your site a better ranking in various search engine results, but make sure the people you hire know what they are doing! SEO is about much more than using keywords over and over again. It is a skilled profession and one where the rules (what Google will and won't accept) change all the time. Hire carefully and always, always ask for testimonials and to see samples of previous work.

Alternatively, you can always learn SEO yourself.

The
Right
Structure

When you set up in business for yourself, you have a choice as to what business structure you want to use.

There are three alternatives available to you as a start-up company:

- Sole trader

- Partnership

- Limited Company

Sole Trader

A sole trader is the easiest of all structures. You work for and by yourself. You alone are entitled to the profits and you alone are responsible for the debts.

There is a guide to the advantages of setting up a sole trader and the steps involved in doing so here: http://www.businesslink.gov.uk/static/html/layer-357.html

To set up as a sole trader you simply need to register your new business with the HMRC. http://www.hmrc.gov.uk/selfemployed/

As a sole trader you will need to pay tax (once a year) and pay National Insurance Contributions Class 2 and Class 4.

You will need to complete a tax return at the end of the tax year and pay tax on your earnings in the previous tax year. When you pay your tax you will also need to pay your Class 4 National Insurance Contributions. You will pay Class 2 NI contributions every quarter.

The HMRC has lots of useful courses and videos on becoming self-employed that you might find useful, explaining accounts, keeping records, legal issues etc. This is a very handy page for women starting up their own business.

Partnership

If you are starting out in business as a partnership, you and your partner are both legally responsible for the debts of the business and also share the profits of the business in proportion to your partnership agreement.

You will need a solicitor to draw up a partnership agreement. You can find advice on setting up in business as a partnership here:

http://www.businesslink.gov.uk/static/html/layer-358.html

You will still pay tax once a year and both Class 2 and Class 4 National Insurance Contributions.

Limited Liability Partnership (LLP)

This structure offers partnerships a limit to the amount of debt they, as partners, are liable for. There is advice on how to set up a limited liability partnership (LLP) here:

http://www.businesslink.gov.uk/static/html/layer-360.html

Limited Company

If you wish to set up your business as a limited company then this is a lot more involved than setting up as a sole trader or partnership. A limited company is a legal entity. This means that the company is responsible for its debts and the company, not you, makes the profit and pays the taxes. The company then pays you a wage or salary or bonus and you will pay tax on that.

Your Limited Company needs to be incorporated with Companies House. You will need a Memorandum of Association and an Articles of Association and to fill in lots of forms! You can find a guide to setting up as a limited company here: http://www.businesslink.gov.uk/static/html/layer-360.html

You can buy a 'off the shelf' company and just change the name with Companies House and this is a quicker way of setting up a limited company. Here are a few of the better known companies offering this service:

http://www.companyregistration.uk-plc.net

http://www.ltd-companies.co.uk/

http://www.paramountformations.com

Accounts and Records

No matter what structure you choose for your business, you will need to keep some basic financial records.

If you are a sole-trader or a partnership, a simple spreadsheet program or cash book will suffice. Keep an accurate record of your incomings and expenses and all receipts relevant to your business and use these to help you complete your tax return.

And when it comes to invoicing your clients, there are several free online invoicing programs you can use to produce invoices and keep track of your business receipts and expenses.

Some highly recommended ones used by women in business are:

- Freshbooks
  http://www.freshbooks.com/uk

- NCH Software
  http://www.nchsoftware.com/invoice/index.html

- QuickBooks
  http://www.intuit.co.uk/

Accurate records will also be handy when it comes to business banking or asking for a business loan.

If you are a limited liability partnership or limited company, you will need an accountant to prepare your accounts for you. Business lenders and business bank managers will expect to see accounts for limited companies.

If you are thinking of hiring an accountant or are confused about financial records I look at record keeping, when to hire an accountant and how to find the best one for you in my workshop.

Business Plans
and
Getting Funding

Business plans sound scary. I don't know why that is but it's true!

A business plan is simply a plan for what you want your business to achieve. It is a road map - a guide to where you are going and a way to keep your business on track. It is also a tracker - a way of measuring your success against your planned targets.

It can be as simple as a list of goals on the back of an envelope or as complicated as a multi-page, multi-referenced report. Most, however, fall somewhere between the two.

Think of it as a way of explaining to someone exactly what your business does and what you intend to achieve in the next three months, six months, year.

You need to write your business plan as soon as you've chosen your name and before you actually start work! The business plan keeps you on track, keeps you focussed and can even help with raising funding.

There is a great video on why you should have a business plan produced by Business Link here:

http://www.businesslink.gov.uk/static/html/hub Chassis-13.html

How to Write a Business Plan

You business plan needs to have the following sections:

- **Executive Summary**

  (What your business does, where the market opportunity is, who you expect your clients to be, when you expect to make a profit). The summary basically sums up everything you've written in the business plan, which is why it makes sense to write this section last.

- **The Business Opportunity**

  -which you are exploiting with your business. Why you are setting up your business.

- **Your Marketing Strategy**

  - how you are going to attract your clients, how you are going to set your rates, what rates you will charge etc.

- **Your Skills**

  - (and in the case of a partnership or limited company - the skills of any staff you will or need to recruit.)

- **Your Place of Operations**

  - Where you will be based, cost of any equipment needed etc.

- **Financial Forecasts**

  - how well you expect to do.

You can find several excellent guides to producing business plans online. Business Link in particular has a very detailed section on this and even offers a template you can download.

http://www.businesslink.gov.uk/static/html/detail-1126.html

For more personal advice and help with business planning, do note that I go through them in detail in my workshop.

Getting Funding

I'm not going to lie to you; the days of easy credit are over and it is hard, very hard to get funding for new businesses these days. But that doesn't mean it is impossible.

As long as you have a good business plan and have obviously researched your market, you might be able to raise a business loan from your local bank. Be sure, however, that you know exactly what it is you are using the loan to do and have worked out your financial targets and can afford the repayments.

You can still get funding from people known as 'Angels' who invest in new businesses and start-ups. In some sectors and parts of the country, you might even be able to get hold of a grant to help you start up your business.

Your local business link might be able to help you when it comes to finance too, by letting you know if you are entitled to a grant.

http://www.businesslink.gov.uk/static/html/layer -42.html

And this site also lists grants available for business too:

http://www.j4b.co.uk/

I talk about ways to get funding on my workshop, but in the meantime you might find this site a handy source of funding information and options:

http://www.startups.co.uk/business-financing?intTrk=topNav

Get the Right Support

So, you've written your plan, got your name and website sorted, chosen the right business structure for you - so now the real work begins!

And now, more so than at the beginning - you need a support network.

You need people to realize that starting up your own business is not like starting any other job. It can take over your life.

You need to put the hours in (where you can) and work hard at getting your business up and running.

You need to ensure your family and friends are aware of this and are aware that when you are 'at work' you are 'at work' even if you're sat in a corner of the kitchen hooked up to the internet.

Plus you need support from other local and national business women, women who've been there and know what you're going through. You need a support network.

If you come to my workshop, you will meet a group of women who are in exactly the same position as you; women who are taking control of their lives and setting up their own business.

But in case you can't get to one of my workshops, here are some links to other organisations especially set up to support women in business.

- Everywoman - Advancing Women in Business
  http://www.everywoman.com/

- Prowess -The UK Online Centre for Women in Business

http://www.prowess.org.uk/

- The Women in Business Network
  http://www.wibn.co.uk/

- Herbusiness
  http://www.herbusinessuk.co.uk/

- OneWomanBusiness
  http://www.onewomanbusiness.co.uk/

Don't overlook other sources of support such as

- HMRC website
  http://www.hmrc.gov.uk/selfemployed/

- Business Link
  http://www.businesslink.gov.uk/static/html/intro.html

Where to Work?

Depending upon the business you choose to set up, you might not need a dedicated office or workspace to begin with. Many self-employed business women work from home from a dedicated space within their home.

Others, such as dog walkers, personal trainers and mobile hair and beauty technicians work outside or in their clients' homes.

If you can work from home when starting out, it will save you quite a bit of money and enable your business to start to earn some profit.

Naturally, this depends upon the type of business you are in and any Health or Safety Laws that might apply. For example there are strict laws regarding food preparation that would also apply to a cake decorator or sandwich maker.

For advice on Health and Safety advice, consult the Health and Safety Executive :

http://www.hse.gov.uk/simple-health-safety/index.htm

Working at Home - The Basics

Depending upon your business you will need the following basics to enable you to work successfully at home:

- A dedicated workspace - this could be a table, a desk or even a home office

- A computer for your work

- An internet connection

- A comfortable chair

- A phone line

- Your business stationery essentials - diary, notepad, calculator, and client files etc.

Wherever you work, make sure you can do so undisturbed!

Later you might decide you need a separate office for your business.

Working outside the Home

If you are looking to rent a space outside your home to work, talk to commercial landlords to find a suitable property to rent.

Here is a handy video from Business link to help you if you need to work outside the home. http://www.businesslink.gov.uk/static/html/hub Chassis-26.html

If you attend my workshop we look into the whole "Where to work" question in a great deal of detail.

Getting
the
Balance Right

Ask anyone who has set up her own business and she will tell you, "It's like having another baby."

Your business can take over your whole life if you let it.

Unlike any normal job or even career, when you start up your own business, it consumes you, it obsesses you and you think about it almost all the time!

This is natural and okay for a short while, but let it continue and you'll soon feel the effects: lethargy, despondency, stress, depression and burn-out.

You must get the balance, the work-life balance right.

You can work 24 hours a day on your business, but you shouldn't. You need to balance your work, your family and your free time.

This is hard! Much harder than when you were in a paid, salaried job!

Here are seven simple tips on how to keep your work-life balance healthy and how to grow your business in a healthy, safe way.

1. Try to keep regular hours.

2. Take regular short breaks away from your work.

3. Get some fresh air and sunshine (if you can!)

4. Keep your work and your family life separate (especially if you have children

- keep making time for them - that is one of the reasons you've set up your own business!)

5. Take holidays!

6. Get some exercise!

7. Eat healthily - it gives you more energy and enables you to focus more.

I go into more detail on managing the Work-Life balance as a self-employed businesswoman in my workshop.

Networking
and
Social Media

Let me let you into a secret... in business it is still very much who you know. But here's the great news...you can soon become a part of this exclusive network. You get to know people by networking with them. Networking both online and offline is a major key to building a successful business. People get scared by networking, but it isn't that scary.

Networking involves meeting other business people and letting them know what you do. That's it. And what's more, most networking takes place in an unthreatening, social setting.

Things like joining your local Chamber of Commerce and attending breakfast meetings, joining national or local women in business groups and attending their events. It is going out, meeting people, making friends and acquaintances.

That's offline networking. Online - we need to use social media. Twitter, LinkedIn, Plaxo, Facebook, Pinterest, forums on business sites - this is where you network online.

This really is crucial for your success in business. I do spend a lot of time talking about this in my workshop as it is an area where most women in business need the most help.

In case you can't make it to my workshop, here are some resources to get you started:

- Facebook Guide to Social Media for Small Businesses: http://www.facebook.com/dellsocialmedia

- 8 Social Media Tips for Small Businesses
  http://www.socialmediaexaminer.com/8-small-business-social-media-tips-from-the-pros/

- And this fantastic pdf "Let's Talk Social Media for Small Businesses"
  http://www.socialmediaexaminer.com/8-small-business-social-media-tips-from-the-pros/

Useful Resources
for Women
in Business

I do hope you can make it to one of my workshops where I can help you face-to-face in your quest to start up your own business. But just in case you can't, here are some more resources from around the world and around the web that you might find useful:

HMRC Self-Employed Pages

http://www.hmrc.gov.uk/selfemployed/

Business Link

http://www.businesslink.gov.uk/static/html/intro.html

Chamber of Commerce

http://www.britishchambers.org.uk/

Westpac

Advice for women setting up in business from an Australian Bank, Westpac, but which is open to women in business everywhere:

http://www.westpac.com.au/business-banking/women-in-business/the-ruby-connection/

Women Home Business

A site and forum from America:

http://www.womenhomebusiness.com/category/working-from-home

Small Business Notes - Women in Small Business

Another resource site from America

http://www.smallbusinessnotes.com/small-business-resources/women-in-small-business.html

Women Business Momentum Centre

A free guide to marketing from the Women Business Momentum Centre - another American organisation

http://womensbusinessmomentum.net/

UK Women's Business Networks

Everywoman - Advancing Women in Business

http://www.everywoman.com

Prowess -The UK Online Centre for Women in Business

http://www.prowess.org.uk/

The Women in Business Network

http://www.wibn.co.uk/

Herbusiness

http://www.herbusinessuk.co.uk/

OneWomanBusiness

http://www.onewomanbusiness.co.uk/

Small Business Set-Ups

Start-ups.co.uk

http://www.startups.co.uk/

Small business.co.uk

http://www.smallbusiness.co.uk/

Contact Berni

If you would like more information about my workshop for women starting out in business, please contact me at berni@first4admin.co.uk. I look forward to hearing from you.

Berni

www.first4admin.co.uk

Facebook:

http://www.facebook.com/First4Admin?ref=ts&f ref=ts

Twitter:

https://twitter.com/first4adm

Linkedin:

uk.linkedin.com/pub/berni-jones/10/5/b42